Let Nothing Disturb You

Let Nothing Disturb You

Teresa of Avila

Series Editor, John Kirvan

Ave Maria Press AVE Notre Dame, Indiana

Series Editor for 30 Days with a Great Spiritual Teacher: John Kirvan.

Originally published as *Let Nothing Disturb You: A Journey to the Center of the Soul with Teresa of Avila* in the 30 Days with a Great Spiritual Teacher series.

———————————————————

Founded in 1865, Ave Maria Press is a ministry of the United States Province of Holy Cross.

www.avemariapress.com

ISBN-10 1-59471-152-6   ISBN-13 978-1-59471-152-7

Cover and text design by Katherine Robinson Coleman.

Printed and bound in the United States of America.

CONTENTS

TIMELINE

1478	The Spanish Inquisition begins, forcing many Muslims and Jews to convert to Christianity. Teresa's paternal grandfather, a wealthy Jewish merchant, is among the converts.
1513	Pope Leo X is elected.
1515	Teresa Sánchez de Cepeda y Ahumada is born in Ávila, Spain, on March 28.
1517	The Protestant Reformation begins with Martin Luther releasing his *Ninety-Five Theses* in Wittenberg, Germany.
1522	Pope Adrian VI is elected.
1523	Pope Adrian VI dies. Pope Clement VII is elected.
ca. 1530	Teresa's mother, Beatriz de Ahumada y Cuevas, dies.
1534	Pope Clement VII dies. Pope Paul III is elected.
1535	Teresa enters the Carmelite Monastery of the Incarnation in Ávila.
1536	Teresa professes her vows.
1536	Teresa becomes deathly ill. During this time, she reads St. Gregory the Great's commentary *Morals on the Book of Job*, and Francis of

Osuna's *Third Spiritual Alphabet*, a book of instructions on spiritual growth, both of which impact her prayer life.

1539   Teresa falls into a coma and is presumed dead. When she comes out of the coma after four days, she learns that her legs are paralyzed. They will remain paralyzed for the next three years, and she will attribute her eventual recovery to St. Joseph's intercession. She begins to have mystical experiences.

1543–1563   The Council of Trent meets in Trent, Italy, in response to the Protestant Reformation and initiates the Counter-Reformation.

1549   Pope Paul III dies.

1550   Pope Julius III is elected.

1554   Teresa experiences healing while praying before a statue of the suffering Christ and senses God's calling while she reads Augustine's *Confessions*. These two events help deepen her mystical communion with God. Some friends and confessors tell her that her mystical experiences were from the devil, while her spiritual advisors and confessors Jesuit Francis Borgia and Franciscan Peter of Alcántra encouraged her.

1555   Pope Julius III dies, and Pope Marcellus II is elected. After Marcellus's death twenty-two days later, Pope Paul IV is elected.

1559   Pope Paul IV dies. Pope Pius IV is elected.

1560   Teresa and a few other Carmelite nuns, dissatisfied with the laxness of their order, begin contemplating and working toward a reform.

1562–1565   Teresa writes *The Book of Her Life*, her spiritual autobiography.

1562   Teresa receives permission from Rome to establish a reformed monastery of Carmelites in Ávila. She dedicates this monastery to St. Joseph. These reformed Carmelites would later be known as Discalced Carmelites.

1562–1569   Teresa writes *The Way of Perfection*.

1565   Pope Pius IV dies.

1566   Pope Pius V is elected.

1567   Teresa writes *Meditations on the Song of Songs*.

1567–1571   The Carmelite General grants Teresa permission to establish more houses of the reformed order. Teresa begins travelling across Spain and establishes reformed convents in Alba de Tormes, Malagón, Medina del Campo, Pastrana, Salamanca, Toledo, and Valladolid.

1568   With the help of Carmelite friars John of the
        Cross and Anthony of Jesus, the first monas-
        tery of reformed orders for brothers is founded
        in Duruelo.

1572   Pope Pius V dies. Pope Gregory XIII is elected.

1573   Teresa writes *The Book of Foundations*, which
        records her travels and work as she established
        reformed convents.

1576   Unreformed Carmelites begin persecuting
        Teresa and her reforms. The governing body
        of Carmelites forbids the establishment of
        additional reformed monasteries and instructs
        Teresa to go into retirement.

1577   Teresa writes *The Interior Castle* as a guide for
        spiritual development through service and
        prayer. The main image of the book is that of
        the soul as a castle made of a single diamond.
        She explores seven mansions within this cas-
        tle and how, through prayer and making one's
        way through these mansions, one can meet
        God in the heart of the castle.

1579   King Philip II of Spain ends the attacks on
        Teresa's friends and associates after receiving
        written appeals from Teresa. As a result, the
        Spanish Inquisition drops the cases against
        Teresa and other reformers.

1580   Pope Gregory XIII issues an edict establishing the reformed Carmelite order as a distinct province of the Carmelites, allowing them to elect their own superiors and author their own constitutions.

1580–1582   Teresa founds convents in Burgos, Granada, Palencia, Soria, and Villanueva de la Jara.

1582   Pope Gregory XIII implements the Gregorian calendar.

1582   Teresa dies in Alba de Tormes, Spain, on October 4 (October 15 in the Gregorian calendar).

1614   Teresa is beatified.

1617   Teresa is proclaimed patroness of Spain.

1622   Teresa is canonized by Pope Gregory XV.

1647–1652   Gian Lorenzo Bernini creates the *Ecstasy of Saint Teresa*, a sculpture based on a vision Teresa had of a seraph driving a fiery lance repeatedly through her heart. The sculpture is located in Santa Maria della Vittoria, Rome, and is one of Bernini's most famous works.

1970   Along with St. Catherine of Siena, Teresa is declared a Doctor of the Church by Pope Paul VI. St. Catherine of Siena and St. Teresa of Avila are the first two women to be named Doctors of the Church.

TERESA OF AVILA

There must have been many days when Teresa of Avila, one of history's great authorities on contemplative prayer, sat—or knelt—without regard for time in the ecstatic silence of a convent cell overlooking a tranquil sixteenth-century Spanish garden.

But read her autobiography and other accounts of her life, and you begin to wonder where she ever found any time to pray or study, where she ever found the space in which to be wrapped in the silence of which she so often speaks, to be caught up in an overwhelming sense of God's love and presence.

So pressured was she that comparisons with the demands made on today's women come quickly and easily to mind.

In a period of about twenty years, beginning when she was in her mid-forties, she wrote five spiritual classics including her *Autobiography, The Way of Perfection* and *The Interior Castle.*

In that same period she carried out a difficult and travel-intensive reform of the long-established religious life of the Carmelite order. It required extraordinary spiritual courage and leadership. But it also required her to become immersed not only in the most basic physical details of daily Carmelite life, but also in the exasperating ecclesiastical and civil politics of over a dozen convents for women and two for men. More often than not she carried out this program in the face

of strenuous opposition—including lawsuits—from both
local and upper-level religious authorities—and even
from the "neighbors" who were often hostile to the
establishment of new religious houses in their area.
Add to all this the fact that she was never in good
health. As an adult she continued to suffer ill-effects of
youthful illnesses. In her early life she had spent days
in a coma and years paralyzed.

Teresa attempted to establish a monastic life suitable to those who, like herself, sought to follow "a more
perfect way" than was being demanded and practiced in
the convent life of her time. We might wonder what sus-
tained her through all the difficulties she faced.

Her own answer is prayer—prayer when it seems
impossible, prayer when others do everything to dis-
suade you and shake your confidence in it, prayer
when you are not sure whether you are being led by
God or by a devil. For everyone who told Teresa that
she was being blessed by God, there was someone with
equal authority telling her that her experiences were
the work of Satan. But she never stopped praying. Her
spiritual teaching was in fact based on two wide-ranging
and provocative metaphors for the life of prayer.

Her first metaphor draws upon the image of the various sources of water needed to irrigate a garden. Teresa
compares the early stages of prayer—our first efforts to
shake off sin and begin to meditate—with the great
effort required to carry a bucket of water on our shoul-
ders from a distant well. As our prayer-life matures, we

enter a phase which she calls the prayer of quiet, a gift-
ed stage of prayer in which we experience God as the
active one while we are more passive. We no longer
struggle to carry the water; it is as if a pump were carry-
ing it to us. In the next stage, a period of dryness, we
discover that we need not draw water from afar, but that
there has been a hidden river present all along from
which we can water our garden. And in our final stage
of growth, we experience God pouring grace upon us,
uniting us with God's own divine life. It is as if bountiful
rain is falling on us.

Teresa's second metaphor views our soul as an interior castle, in the very center of which dwells the Holy
Trinity. Growth in prayer enables us to enter into an
ever deeper intimacy with God—signified by a progres-
sive journey through the apartments (or mansions) of
the castle, from outermost sections to the luminous
center. When we have attained union with God, to the
fullest degree possible to us in this life, we have arrived
at the center of ourselves. We enjoy integrity as human
beings and as children of God. Each of the mansions
represents a different stage in the evolution of our
prayer life. As we enter each new mansion, we experience the effect of this new stage in every other phase of
our life.

Both metaphors pick us up at the beginning of our
search for union with God. Neither stops short of
the most perfect union possible in this life, union
with divinity.

But however sophisticated and rarefied her spiritual experience and writing, however lofty and apparently exotic her expectations, her spiritual life, example, and teaching were rooted in some very basic truths. These apply to us, however primitive and stumbling our spiritual efforts, however limited our vision.

No matter what happens, do not stop praying.

Never forget that no two of us ever travel exactly the same spiritual path.

And, as she was wont to remind us, do not expect an easy journey. Reflecting on the difficult path that Jesus walked, and on her own trials, she is reported to have said to God: "If this is the way you treat your friends, it's no wonder you have so few!"

This small book is neither a theological or historical compendium, nor a guide to Teresa's spiritual theories. It is a series of meditations drawn from her various works written at difficult times in her life. Each one seeks to substantiate the spiritual wisdom of her advice to let nothing disturb us—especially in our attempts to pray and to find our own special paths. We will focus not so much on the great metaphors of her major works, but on the underlying truths that illumine the journey to the center of the soul—hers and ours.

HOW TO PRAY
THIS BOOK

The purpose of this book is to open a gate for you, to make accessible the spiritual experience and wisdom of one of history's most important spiritual teachers, Teresa of Avila.

This is not a book for mere reading. It invites you to meditate and pray its words on a daily basis over a period of thirty days.

It is a handbook for a spiritual journey.

Before you read the "rules" for taking this spiritual journey, remember that this book is meant to free your spirit, not confine it. If on any day the meditation does not resonate well for you, turn elsewhere to find a passage which seems to best fit the spirit of your day and your soul. Don't hesitate to repeat a day as often as you like until you feel that you have discovered what the Spirit, through the words of the author, has to say to your spirit.

Here are suggestions on one way to use this book as a cornerstone of your prayers.

As Your Day Begins

As the day begins, set aside a quiet moment in a quiet place to read the meditation suggested for the day.

The passage is short. It never runs more than a couple of hundred words, but it has been carefully selected to give a spiritual focus, a spiritual center to your whole day. It is designed to remind you as another day begins of your own existence at a spiritual level. It is meant to put you in the presence of the spiritual master who is your companion and teacher on this journey. But most of all, the purpose of the passage is to remind you that at this moment and at every moment during this day, you will be living and acting in the presence of a God who invites you continually, but quietly, to live in and through him.

A word of advice: read slowly. Very slowly. The meditation has been broken into sense lines to help you do just this. Don't read to get to the end, but to savor each part of the meditation. You never know what short phrase, what word will trigger a response in your spirit. Give the words a chance. After all, you are not just reading this passage, you are praying it. You are establishing a mood of serenity for your whole day. What's the rush?

ALL THROUGH YOUR DAY

Immediately following the day's reading you will find a single sentence that we call a mantra, a word borrowed from the Hindu tradition. This phrase is meant as a companion for your spirit as it moves through a busy day. Write it down on a 3" x 5" card or on the appropriate page of your daybook. Look at it as often as you can. Repeat it quietly to yourself and go on your way.

It is not meant to stop you in your tracks or to distract you from responsibilities, but simply, gently, to remind you of the presence of God and your desire to respond to this presence.

As Your Day Is Ending

This is a time for letting go of the day.

Find a quiet place and quiet your spirit. Breathe deeply. Inhale, exhale—slowly and deliberately again and again until you feel your body let go of its tension.

Now read the evening prayer slowly, phrase by phrase. You may recognize at once that we have taken one of the most familiar evening prayers of the Christian tradition and woven into it phrases taken from the meditation with which you began your day and the mantra that has accompanied you all through your day. In this way, a simple evening prayer gathers together the spiritual character of the day that is now ending as it began—in the presence of God.

It is a time for summary and closure.

Invite God to embrace you with love and to protect you through the night.

Sleep well.

Some Other Ways to Use This Book

1. Use it any way your spirit suggests. As mentioned earlier, skip a passage that doesn't resonate for you on a given day, or repeat for a second day or even several days a passage whose richness speaks to you. The truths of a spiritual life are not absorbed in

a day or, for that matter, in a lifetime. So take your time. Be patient with the Lord. Be patient with yourself.

2. Take two passages and/or their mantras—the more contrasting the better—and "bang" them together. Spend time discovering how their similarities or differences illumine your path.

3. Start a spiritual journal to record and deepen your experience of this thirty-day journey. Using either the mantra or another phrase from the reading that appeals to you, write a spiritual account of your day, a spiritual reflection. Create your own meditation.

4. Join millions who are seeking to deepen their spiritual life by joining with others to form small groups. More and more people are doing just this to support each other in their mutual quest. Meet once a week or at least every other week to discuss and pray about one of the meditations. There are many books and guides available to help you make such a group effective.

John Kirvan, Series Editor

THIRTY DAYS WITH

TERESA OF AVILA

DAY ONE

••

My Day Begins

A whole lifetime is short,
and sometimes very short indeed.
How do we know that ours may not be so short
as to end an hour,
or even a minute after
we have determined to give ourselves wholly to God?
It is quite possible,
for we cannot depend on anything
that passes away,
much less on life,
on which we must not reckon
for even a single day.
We may be among those who,
worldly as we still are,
have some deep desire
to do what is right.
At times, rare as they may be,
we commend ourselves to God's care.
We think about our souls every now and then.

Busy as we are,
we pray a few times a month,
even though our minds are filled
with a thousand other matters.
"Where your treasure is, there also is your heart."
We need, therefore, from time to time
to cast aside our daily concerns.
We need to reflect upon the state of our soul,
and to realize
that we will never reach our goal
by the road we are following.
We need to withdraw from time to time
from all unnecessary cares and business.

ALL THROUGH THE DAY

A whole lifetime is short.
I cannot depend on anything that passes away.

MY DAY IS ENDING

Let nothing, O Lord,
disturb the silence of this night.
Let nothing make me afraid.
For even though life is short,

even though it could end before I wake,
if I put all my trust in you,
and not in passing things,
I need not be concerned.
Let me now,
in the dying moments of this day,
cast aside my concerns
and reflect upon the state of my soul.
Worldly as I still am,
I harbor a deep desire
to do what is right
and to commend myself
wholly to your care.
For if I have you, God,
I will want for nothing.
You alone suffice.

DAY TWO

....

My Day Begins

We hear the Lord calling to us
and promising us his peace,
even when we are still caught up
in the pleasures and vanities of this world.
But so desirous is our Lord
that we should seek him
and enjoy the peace of his company,
that in one way or another
he never ceases calling to us.

However slow we are to answer,
however unable or unwilling we are
to do his bidding at once,
we need not be downcast or discouraged.
God is willing to wait for us for many a day,
and even many a year,
especially when perseverance
and good desires are in our hearts.
Perseverance is our essential first response
to God's invitation to peace of soul.

What need we have of God's mercy,
lest the easy attractions of the world
delude us into forsaking
what we have so tentatively begun,
lest we fail to persevere
in our desire to answer God's invitation to peace.
We need to persevere
in our desire to love the Lord
and in our attempts to make some return to him
for so many proofs of his love,
especially his constant, persevering presence
in our soul.
This faithful lover never gives up on us.

However long we live,
we could never wish
for a better friend than God,
who even in this life
grants us a far greater peace
than we are able to desire.

ALL THROUGH THE DAY

God is willing to wait for me
for many a day, even many a year.

MY DAY IS ENDING

Let nothing, O Lord,
disturb the silence of this night.
Let nothing make me afraid.
I hear you, O Lord, calling to me
and promising me your peace,
even though I am still caught up
in the pleasures and vanities of this world.
But so much do you desire
that I should seek you
and enjoy the peace of your company,
that in one way or another
you never cease calling to me.
You have willingly waited for me
for many a day,
and even many a year.
I have been, I know, slow to answer,
unable and unwilling
to do your bidding at once.

But I need not be downcast or discouraged
if you can find in my heart
perseverance and desire
to respond to your invitation
to peace of soul.
For if I have you, God,
I will want for nothing.
You alone suffice.

DAY THREE

··

MY DAY BEGINS

I believe the Lord helps those
who set out to do great things for his sake
and never fails those who trust in him alone,
who depend on him to meet all their needs.
This does not mean
that I am excused from seeking to help myself,
only that in trusting him I will be free from anxiety.

I prefer to have around me
people who help me to believe that this is so.
I try to surround myself
with people who seem to be making great progress
in the love and service of God,
with those who place their trust in God alone.
I seek out those who are
single-minded and courageous
in their desire to do great things for the Lord,
and who place all their trust in him.
Do as I do,
and you will find that they will be a great help to you

as they are to me.
Avoid being around the timid,
those who appear to be making only halfhearted
attempts to help themselves,
and who place only halfhearted trust in God.

As for yourself,
"Do not be anxious
about what you are to eat and put on,"
but leave it to God.
May God grant you, as he has granted me,
the gift of freedom from anxiety.

ALL THROUGH THE DAY

Do not be anxious
about what you are to eat or to put on,
but leave it to God.

MY DAY IS ENDING

Let nothing, O Lord,
disturb the silence of this night.
Let nothing make me afraid.
Reassure me at the end of this day
that you will help me

as you help all those
who set out to do great things for your sake.
You never fail those
who trust in you alone,
who depend on you
to meet all their needs.
I will not, with your help,
be anxious
about what I am to eat and put on,
but leave it to you, God.
Grant me, as you granted Teresa,
the gift of freedom from anxiety.
For if I have you, God,
I will want for nothing.
You alone suffice.

DAY FOUR

....

MY DAY BEGINS

I cannot understand why it is
that people are afraid to set out
on the road to perfection.

Whoever truly loves you, my God,
travels by a broad and a royal road,
travels securely
far away from any precipice.
Hardly do we stumble,
even in the slightest degree,
when you, O Lord, give us your hand.
One fall—even many falls—
if we love you
and not the things of this world,
will not be enough to lead us to perdition.
We will be traveling along the valley of humility.
May the Lord
make us realize how unsafe we are
amid such manifest perils as beset us
when we follow the crowd,

and how our true safety
lies in striving to press ever forward
on the way of God.
Our eyes must be fixed upon our goal.
We must not be afraid
that this Sun of Justice will set,
or that God will allow us to travel by night,
and so be lost,
unless we first choose to forsake the journey
we have begun.

ALL THROUGH THE DAY

Anyone who truly loves God
travels securely.

MY DAY IS ENDING

Let nothing, O Lord,
disturb the silence of this night.
Let me not be afraid
to set out on the road to perfection.
If I truly love you, my God,
I will travel securely by a broad and royal road,
far from any precipice.
If I stumble, even in the slightest,

you will be there, I know,
to reach out your hand
and catch me before I fall completely.
Remind me again, as this day ends,
how unsafe I am
when I follow the crowd,
and how truly secure I am
when I press ever forward toward you.
For if I have you, God,
I will want for nothing.
You alone suffice.

DAY FIVE

....

MY DAY BEGINS

More courage is required
of those who set out on the road to perfection
than of those who suddenly become a martyr,
for perfection is not attained overnight.

You have yet to conquer your passions.
Yet by the very fact that you seek to love God,
you expect to be extremely brave,
as brave as a great saint.
You find yourself praising the Lord,
but at the same time knowing deep sadness of soul.
Many turn back at this point
because they have no idea
how to help themselves.

Many souls desire to fly
before God gives them wings.
They begin with good desires,
with great fervor and determination
to advance in virtue.

Some actually give up all things
for the sake of God.
Then they see in others who are further along the way
great virtues to which they can only aspire.
They read books about prayer and contemplation,
about all they must do
to achieve their spiritual goals,
and they lose heart.

Do not be troubled, but hope in the Lord.
For if you desire to do the will of the Lord,
if you pray and hope in the Lord
and do what you can for yourself
God will bring about in your soul
all that you desire.
It is very, very important that our weak natures
should have great confidence,
and not be dismayed.
We should think that if we do our best,
we will be victorious.

ALL THROUGH THE DAY

Let me not try to fly before God gives me wings.

MY DAY IS ENDING

Let nothing, O Lord,
disturb the silence of this night.
Let nothing make me afraid.
Especially as this day ends, remind me
that perfection is not attained overnight.
I know that if I desire to do your will, O Lord,
if I pray and hope in you
and do what I can for you,
you will bring about in my soul all that you desire.
It is very, very important, I know,
that my weak nature
should have great confidence in you,
and not be dismayed.
If I do my best,
I will be victorious.
I will fly,
but not before you give me wings.
Grant me patience.
Let me not turn back now.
For if I have you, God,
I will want for nothing.
You alone suffice.

DAY SIX

MY DAY BEGINS

Our Lord asks but two things of us:
love for God,
and love for our neighbor.
These are the two virtues
that we must strive to obtain.
If we practice them perfectly
we shall be doing the will of God,
and so will find the union we seek.
The most certain sign
that we keep these two commandments
is that we have a genuine love for each other.
We may not know for certain whether we love God,
but there can be no doubt
about whether or not we love our neighbor.

If we fail to love our neighbor,
we are deceiving ourselves
if we think that we love God.

But if we possess a true love of neighbor
we will certainly attain to union with our Lord.

Beg God to grant you true love of others
and you will be rewarded with more
than you know how to desire.
God will insist that you surrender your self-interests
for those of your neighbor,
taking upon yourself their burdens.

Do not believe that this will cost you nothing
and that you will find it all done for you by God.
Never forget what the love God bore for all of us
cost the Son of God.
To free others—his neighbors—from death,
he suffered the most painful death of all,
the death of the cross.

ALL THROUGH THE DAY

Love your neighbor as you love yourself.

My Day Is Ending

Let nothing, O Lord,
disturb the silence of this night.
Let nothing make me afraid.
Let me wake refreshed,
ready to love and care for my neighbor
as you have loved and cared for me,
and indeed as I love and care for myself.
For if I do not love others
I cannot fool myself into believing
that I love you.
I am, I know, as this day ends
very far from such a love.
But hear my prayer.
When I see others,
let me see you.
Let me show them
the same reverence and respect
that I would show you.
If I love them,
I will love you.
and I will want for nothing.

DAY SEVEN

··

MY DAY BEGINS

You do not have to be bashful with God
as some people are,
in the belief that they are being humble.
It would not be humility on your part
if your sovereign were to do you a favor,
and you refused to accept it.
But you would be showing humility
by taking it and being pleased with it,
yet realizing how far you are from deserving it.

A fine humility it would be
if I had the royalty of heaven and earth in my house,
coming to it to do me a favor
and to delight in my company,
and I were so humble
that I would not answer their questions,
or remain with my guests,
or accept their gifts, but left them alone.
A fine humility it would be
if they were to speak to me

and beg me to ask for what I wanted,
and I were so humble
that I preferred to remain poor
and even let them go away,
so that they would see I had not sufficient resolution.
Have nothing to do with that kind of humility.
Speak with God as a father, as a mother,
as a brother, as a sister,
as a lord, as a spouse.
Sometimes in one way,
sometimes in another, God will teach you
what you must do to be pleasing.
Do not be foolish.
Ask permission to speak
with the spouse of your soul.
Remember how important it is
for you to have understood this truth—
the Lord is within us
and we should be aware of his presence.

All Through the Day

Do not be bashful with God.

MY DAY IS ENDING

Let nothing, O Lord,
disturb the silence of this night.
Let nothing make me afraid.
For you are with me,
and I am with you.
Let me not be shy in your presence.
Rather let me speak with you
in confidence, trust, and love.
For you are my father and mother,
my brother and sister,
my lord, my spouse.
In whatever way pleases you,
teach me what I must do to please you.
However undeserving I am,
I humbly ask you
to fill this night
with the gifts of your love,
with the gift of yourself.
For if I have you, God,
I will want for nothing.
You alone suffice.

DAY EIGHT

....

My Day Begins

We pray to our Father "who art in heaven."
But where is heaven?
Where shall we find our Father?
It is important to know and experience
the answer to this question
if we are to concentrate our minds and souls.

You know that God is everywhere;
and this is a great truth,
for, of course, wherever God is, there is heaven.
No doubt you can believe
that in any place where his majesty is,
there is fullness of glory.
Remember how St. Augustine tells us
about his seeking God in many places
and eventually finding his father within himself.
Do you suppose it is of little importance
that a soul that is easily distracted
should come to understand this truth,
and to find that, in order to speak to its eternal father

and to take delight in him,
it has no need to go to heaven
or to speak in a loud voice?
However quietly we speak,
God is so near that we will be heard.
We need no wings to go in search of God,
but have only to find a place where we can be alone
and look upon the presence within us.
Nor need we feel strange
in the presence of so great a guest.
We must talk with God humbly.
We should speak with our father
and ask for whatever we would ask of a father
or mother.
We should spell out our troubles
and beg to have them put right;
and at the same time realize
we are not worthy to be the children of God.

ALL THROUGH THE DAY

No matter how quietly I speak, God hears.

My Day Is Ending

Let nothing, O Lord,
disturb the silence of this night.
Let nothing make me afraid.
Here in the dark
remind me that in order to speak to you
my eternal father
and to take delight in you,
I have no need to go to heaven
or to speak in a loud voice.
However quietly I speak,
you are so near that you will hear me.
I need no wings to go in search of you,
but have only to understand
that the quiet of this night
is a place where I can be alone with you
and look upon your presence with me.
For if I have you, God,
I want for nothing.
You alone suffice.

DAY NINE

MY DAY BEGINS

We are so far from esteeming highly enough
our soul in which God so delights.
Each of us possesses a soul,
but we do not realize its value
as made in the image of God;
therefore we fail to understand
the great secrets it contains.
If we reflect, we shall see that our soul
is a paradise in which
God takes delight.

Let us think of our soul
as resembling a castle
formed of a single diamond,
or a very transparent crystal
containing many rooms,
of which some are above,
some below, others at the side.
In the center,
in the very midst of them all,

is the principal chamber,
in which God and our soul
hold their most secret intercourse.
What do you imagine
that dwelling to be,
in which a king, so mighty, so wise, and so pure—
containing all good—
can come to rest?

Nothing can be compared to
the great beauty and capabilities of our soul.
However keen our intellects be,
we are no more able
to comprehend the depths of our soul
than we are able to comprehend God,
for our soul has been created
in the image and likeness of God.
It is our soul's likeness to God
that makes it possible for us
to commune with the God in whose image
we have been made.

ALL THROUGH THE DAY

You take delight in my soul.

MY DAY IS ENDING

Let nothing, O Lord,
disturb the silence of this night.
Let nothing make me afraid.
Rather, as darkness descends
and this day ends,
let me retreat to the very center of my being,
to my soul,
which you, my heavenly father,
have created in your own image and likeness
and which you have chosen as your home.
Make me aware of your presence
and of my likeness to you.
Let us speak together in the silence of the night.
If indeed my soul is a paradise
in which you take your delight,
let me find my delight in your presence.
For if I have you, God,
I will want for nothing.
You alone suffice.

DAY TEN

My Day Begins

I think often of St. Paul's words that
"all things are possible in God."

As you set out on your journey
take no notice of the warnings people give you,
or the dangers they suggest.
It is absurd to think
that you can travel along a road full of bandits
to reach a costly treasure
without running any risks.
The worldly think that happiness consists
of journeying peacefully through life.
Yet for the sake of making an extra dollar
they will sacrifice their sleep night after night,
and leave others with no peace of mind or body.

You are traveling by the royal and safe road
along which our Lord,
all the elect, and the saints have passed.
Put aside the misgivings

that the world would impose upon you.
Take no notice of public opinion.
This is no time to believe everything you hear.
Be guided only by those who conform their lives
to the will of God.
Try to keep a good conscience.
Practice humility.
Despise the values of the world.
Do these things
and you can be sure
that you are on the right road.

If God is pleased with you,
whoever resists you—
whoever they might be—
will be utterly disappointed.

ALL THROUGH THE DAY

All things are possible in God.

MY DAY IS ENDING

Let nothing, O Lord,
disturb the silence of this night.

Let nothing make me afraid.
Silence the voices
that would discourage me
from following the royal road of perfection
along which your own Son
and all the saints have traveled.
My happiness will consist
not in untroubled, peaceful days,
but in the courage to follow your will
wherever it may take me.
In your words,
not in public opinion,
I will find my way.
There are risks,
but if I have you, God,
all things are possible.
I will want for nothing.
You alone suffice.

DAY ELEVEN

....

MY DAY BEGINS

When you pray
you may wish to picture yourself
in the presence of Christ
and be caught up
in a great love for his sacred humanity.
You may get used to being in his presence,
to speaking with him,
asking him for things you need,
making your complaints known to him,
telling him of your trials,
but also rejoicing with him in your joys.

Make sure that you never allow
your pleasure in these gifts
to make you forgetful of the Giver.
But this may not happen;
do not be anxious.
There is no need for you
to compose beautifully worded prayers.
Use whatever words suit your needs and desires.

This is an excellent way of making progress in the spiritual life and making it quickly.
But don't spend all your time
summoning up the presence of God.
There is nothing wrong with this method of prayer,
but enjoyable as it is
give your soul an occasional Sunday—
a day of rest from your labor.
Keep yourself in the presence of God,
let your imagination work for you,
but do not weary your mind
or grow tired composing speeches.
Simply set out your needs
and acknowledge that you have no right
to be always aware of God's presence.
There is a time for this,
and a time for that.
Observe them.
Otherwise your soul will grow weary.

ALL THROUGH THE DAY

Do not be anxious.

MY DAY IS ENDING

Let nothing, O Lord,
disturb the silence of this night.
Let nothing make me afraid.
As this day ends and I recall your presence
let me not be anxious
about what I shall say to you.
There is no need, I know,
to compose beautifully worded prayers.
You will hear whatever words I have.
I need not grow exhausted
summoning up your presence,
or weary my mind and grow tired
composing speeches to you.
Let me simply set my needs before you—
making my complaints known to you,
telling you of my trials,
but also rejoicing with you in my joys,
making sure that I never allow
my pleasure in your gifts
to make me forgetful of you the Giver.
For if I have you, God,
I will want for nothing.
You alone suffice.

DAY TWELVE

··

MY DAY BEGINS

May God let you taste
the incredible joy of complete union.
Nothing the world can give us—
not possessions, not riches, not delights or honors, not
great feasts or festivals—
can match the happiness of a single moment
spent by a soul totally united to God.
Nor can any earthly pain or suffering,
any effort or striving on our part,
earn such a loving touch,
so complete a union,
an experience of love so profound.
We cannot, in fact, earn a single hour
of the satisfaction, joy, and delight
that God can bring to our soul.
"All the trials of the world," says St. Paul,
"are not worthy to be compared
with the glory for which we hope."

My merciful and gracious Lord,
what more could I ask of you in this life?
than to be so close to you that there is no separation
between you and me?
Joined to you, what could be difficult?
With you so near
what could I not undertake for your sake?
What am I without you?
What am I worth if I am not near you?
If ever I should stray from you,
even a short way,
how would I ever find myself?

With St. Augustine, I pray fervently:
"Give me what you have chosen for me,
and bring about in me what you desire for me."

Never, with your grace and favor,
will I turn my back on you.

ALL THROUGH THE DAY

What am I without you, Lord?

MY DAY IS ENDING

Let nothing, O Lord,
disturb the silence of this night.
Let nothing make me afraid.
Whatever this day has brought me,
whether joy and satisfaction,
or pain and frustration,
they are not worthy to be compared
with the glory for which we hope.
My merciful and gracious Lord,
what more could I ask of you in this life
than to be so close to you
that there is no separation between you and me?
With St. Augustine, I pray fervently:
"Give me what you have chosen for me,
and bring about in me what you desire for me."
For what am I without you?
What am I worth if I am not near you?
If ever I should stray from you,
even a short distance,
how would I ever find myself?
But if I have you, God,
I will want for nothing.
You alone suffice.

DAY THIRTEEN

....

MY DAY BEGINS

The Lord said to me:
"Very few there are who love me in truth.
For to love me in this way is to know
that everything that is not pleasing to me
is a deception.
But if you love me in truth
I will not hide anything from you."

I see now that it is a great blessing
to set no store by anything that is not true,
anything that is not pleasing to my Lord.

I now look upon anything
that is not directed to the service of God
as vanity and deception.
I have become firmly resolved
to carry out with all my might
even the smallest detail of divine scripture.
I have come to believe
that there is no obstacle that I cannot overcome

in my desire to live in the truth,
to speak only of things that are true,
that is, things that bring us closer to God,
that go far beyond any worldly wisdom.

The Lord has invited us to walk in truth
in the presence of Truth itself.

The truth of which the Lord speaks,
is Truth without beginning or end.
Upon this Truth all other truths depend,
just as all other loves depend on this Love,
and all other greatness upon this Greatness.

For it comes down to this:
The Lord is Truth itself.
All else is a lie.

ALL THROUGH THE DAY

There is no obstacle that I cannot overcome.

MY DAY IS ENDING

Let nothing, O Lord,
disturb the silence of this night.
Let nothing frighten me.
Grant me rest
in the knowledge
that there is no obstacle
to your love
that cannot be overcome,
if I only accept your invitation to walk in truth
in the presence of you who are Truth itself.
Upon you all other truths depend,
just as all other loves depend on your love,
and all other greatness upon your greatness.
As darkness descends
grant me a quiet night.
Place your truth on my lips and in my heart.
For it comes down to this:
You, Lord, are Truth itself.
All else is a lie.

If I speak your truth, O Lord God,
I will want for nothing.
You alone suffice.

DAY FOURTEEN

....

MY DAY BEGINS

Let us learn from this, my brothers and sisters,
that if we would bear any resemblance to our God,
we must strive ever to walk in truth.
I do not mean merely
that we should not tell falsehoods;
I mean rather
that we should act with perfect truth
before God and all persons.
Above all
that we should not wish to be thought
better than we are.
In all our deeds
we should ascribe to God what is God's,
and attribute what is ours to ourselves;
we should seek for truth in all things.
In this way we will care little for the world,
which is built on deception and falsehood
and therefore cannot last.
God grant us
never to lose the grace of self-knowledge.

If for the love of God
we hated honors, possessions, and pleasures,
embraced the cross,
and set about God's service in earnest,
Satan would fly away from such realities
as from a plague.
He is the friend of lies and a lie himself.
He wants nothing to do
with those who walk in truth.

Let us speak
only that which is perfectly true,
and in so doing raise our sights to Truth itself,
that is, to God.

ALL THROUGH THE DAY

Let me walk in truth.

MY DAY IS ENDING

Let nothing, O Lord,
disturb the silence of this night.
Let nothing make me afraid.
Remove the dust of this day.

Forgive my lies,
the dozen ways in which today I have denied
in word and action
that you alone
are the source of all true life.
Cleanse my lips, my heart, my whole life
of the untruths,
the petty pride and self-love
that so easily, so persistently, come between us.
Fill my night with your forgiveness,
with that peace
that is possible only for those
who walk in your truth.

If I walk with you in truth, my Lord God,
I will want for nothing.
You alone are the Truth.
You alone suffice.

DAY FIFTEEN

....

MY DAY BEGINS

The whole foundation of prayer is humility.
The more we humble ourselves in prayer,
the more will God lift us up.

Once, while I was wondering
why our Lord so dearly loves the virtue of humility,
this thought suddenly struck me
without previous reflection:
it is because God is the supreme Truth,
and humility *is* the truth.

It is a basic truth
that of ourselves we are nothing.
Whoever ignores this
lives a life of falsehood.
Those who realize and accept this truth
are the most deeply pleasing to God,
the supreme Truth,
for they walk in truth.

I know a person to whom our Lord revealed
that nothing good in us springs from ourselves.
Rather, it comes from the waters of grace,
near which the soul remains,
like a tree planted by a river,
and from that Sun
which gives life to our works.
Wherever and whenever she saw good,
she turned at once to God as its fountainhead,
without whose help she well knew
we can do nothing.

What wonders we shall see
if we keep before our eyes our frailty and folly,
and recognize
how unworthy we are
to be the servants of so great a Lord,
whose marvels are beyond our comprehension.

ALL THROUGH THE DAY

Humility!

MY DAY IS ENDING

Let nothing, O Lord,
disturb the silence of this night.
Let nothing make me afraid.
Let me go humbly
into the darkness
admitting to myself and to you
that of myself I am nothing.
Let me walk in this hard truth
accepting my own frailty and folly,
even as you open my eyes
to the incomprehensible wonders and marvels
that you have in store
for those who follow you in truth.
I may have nothing of myself,
but if I have you, God,
I will have enough.
You alone suffice.

DAY SIXTEEN

MY DAY BEGINS

The soul that truly loves God
loves all good,
protects all good,
praises all good,
joins itself to good people,
helps and defends them,
and embraces all the virtues.
It loves only what is truly worth loving.

Do you think that it is possible
for anyone who truly loves God,
to care for vanities, riches,
or worldly pleasures and honors?
Such a person cannot quarrel or feel envy,
for she aims at nothing
but pleasing the object of her love.
Whether your love of God is great or small,
it must show itself.
Love for God can never be concealed.

When you love God deeply,
it will be plainly evident in many ways,
for a large fire throws a bright and clear flame.

A love that is strong and just,
that grows for as long as we live,
that there is no reason ever to end,
a love that is returned so fully—
can a love such as this be concealed?

If you ask me how such a love is to be attained,
my answer is:
Resolve firmly to do and suffer for God,
putting your resolution into action
whenever the opportunity occurs.
Your love must not be just something you imagine,
something you desire.
You must prove it by works.

ALL THROUGH THE DAY

Love cannot be hidden.

My Day Is Ending

Let nothing, O Lord,
disturb the silence of this night.
Let nothing make me afraid.
But it is not enough
as night descends
to be here alone with you,
wrapped in your serenity.
My love for you—great or small—
must show itself
whenever the opportunity occurs.
My love must not be
something I just dream about,
something in whose warmth I wrap myself
in the closing hours of the day.
I must prove it by works.
True love goes beyond prayerful words
to loving deeds.
True love for you must not—cannot—be concealed.

If I love you, God,
words will never be enough.
Only if I act on your love
will I want for nothing.
You alone will suffice.

DAY SEVENTEEN

My Day Begins

How is it, O God,
that even when we are determined to love you,
we do not rise immediately
to the perfect love that is our goal?

It is because while we think
we are surrendering all to God,
we are in fact giving up
only the profits of our endeavors,
the extras,
what is left over from our daily needs.
We keep ownership of the land itself.

We resolve to become poor,
and it is a great thing to do.
But we take great care never to be in want,
not just of what is necessary,
but of what is superfluous.

We give up our search for honor.

But the moment our honor is in danger,
we forget that we have given it to God.
We would take back our gift,
snatching it, as it werc,
from the hands of the one to whom we claim
to have surrendered our will.
So it is in so many things.
In everything
we look for pleasant ways of serving God.
And because we do not give up ourselves
wholly and at once,
so the treasure of God's gifts to us
are not given at once.

Heavenly Father,
even as we measure out our lives to you
a bit at a time,
we must be content
to receive your gifts drop by drop,
until we have surrendered our lives wholly to you.

ALL THROUGH THE DAY

Patience gains all things.

MY DAY IS ENDING

Let nothing, O Lord,
disturb the silence of this night.
Let nothing make me afraid.
Let my fears give way
to quiet rest,
and my timidity to generosity of heart.
As much as I say that
I wish to give myself wholly to you,
the truth is
that I measure out the gift of my life
a drop at a time,
hoping however vainly
to find some pleasant, easy,
less than wholehearted way
of coming to know, love, and serve you.
I keep taking back the gift I offer.
Replace, I pray you, my stinginess of heart
with a reflection of your generosity.
You will reward my every gift,
no matter how small,
with the unlimited gift of yourself.
And if I have you, God,
I will want for nothing.
You alone suffice.

DAY EIGHTEEN

My Day Begins

Prayer is the doorway through which
God's greatest gifts enter our soul.
If this door is kept shut,
I do not see how God can bestow these gifts;
for even if God wishes to enter our soul,
to take delight therein,
and to make us also to delight,
there is no way this can be done.
If we want God to come to us,
why would we fail to pray?
Certainly I cannot comprehend it
unless we have a mind
to go through the troubles of this life
in greater misery!

Why would we shut the door in the face of God?
In return for a little effort on our part
God gives us the help we need to bear our trials.

Therefore when God plants in our soul,

a desire to pray,
as unprepared as we might be,
it is among the greatest of gifts.
If we persevere,
in spite of sins, temptations, and relapses,
our Lord will bring us at last
to the harbor of salvation.
Besides, God does not wait for the next life
to reward our love,
but begins to enrich us even here.

A<small>LL</small> T<small>HROUGH THE</small> D<small>AY</small>

Prayer is the doorway through which
God's greatest gifts enter my soul.

M<small>Y</small> D<small>AY</small> I<small>S</small> E<small>NDING</small>

Let nothing, O Lord,
disturb the silence of this night.
Let nothing make me afraid.
Let nothing distract me
from spending
these last moments of the day
with you in prayer.

Help me to open the doorway
through which I can glimpse your presence
and through which
you can enter my soul.
Let me not shut you out.
If only for a moment,
here and now at the end of the day,
let me silence the thousand voices
that kept me through the day
from remembering
that I live always in your presence.
Bless me with the gift of prayer.
With it I have you, God,
I will want for nothing.
You alone suffice.

DAY NINETEEN

∙∙∙

MY DAY BEGINS

Of what does the highest perfection consist?

Do not look for, or expect to find it
in interior delights,
or in great raptures and visions,
or in the gift of prophecy,
but only in conforming our wills
to the will of God.
Then there will be nothing
that God wills
that we do not will ourselves,
and with our whole will.
We will accept the bitter with the sweet,
knowing it to be the will of God.

For the raptures may pass,
leaving only scanty obedience to the will of God.
Self-will will remain, our soul joined to self-love
rather than to the will of God.

Choosing the will of God is very hard to do.
For not only must we choose
to do the will of God,
but we must be pleased with doing
that which, according to our nature,
may be in every way the opposite of
that which we would choose for ourselves.

Certainly this is hard.
But love, if perfect,
is strong enough to do it.

In love, we forget our own pleasure
in order to please the God
who loves us so much.

ALL THROUGH THE DAY

Perfection is not in feeling good,
but in doing the will of God.

MY DAY IS ENDING

Let nothing, O Lord,
disturb the silence of this night.
Let nothing make me afraid.
I come to the end of an ordinary day,
a day when there have been
no overwhelming interior joys,
no great raptures or visions.
There have been bitter moments and sweet.
I have tried to accept whatever came my way,
doing my best
to conform my will
to your will, my Lord God,
so that there would be nothing
that you will
that I would not choose for myself
with my whole will.
For if I have you, God,
I will want for nothing.
You alone suffice.

DAY TWENTY

MY DAY BEGINS

It is a great help in our quest
to have high aspirations,
because often our actions
begin with our thoughts and dreams.
It is not pride to have great desires.
It is the devil who makes us think
that the lives and actions of the saints
are to be admired but not imitated.
If we do not limit our spiritual goals,
we can with great confidence,
little by little, reach those heights
that by the grace of God
many saints have reached.
If they had never resolved to desire,
and had never, little by little,
acted upon that resolve,
they would never have ascended so high.
Like them we need to be humble
but bold in our pursuit,
trusting God and not ourselves.

For our Lord seeks and loves courageous souls.
Let us not fail to reach our spiritual destiny
because we have been too timid,
too cautious in our desires,
because we sought too little.

It is true that I might stumble
for trying to do too much too soon,
but it is also certain that I will never succeed
if I hope for too little,
or out of fear of failing
start not at all.

All Through the Day

Do not hope for too little.

My Day Is Ending

Let nothing, O Lord,
disturb the silence of this night.
Let nothing make me afraid.
As darkness hides me
with no one but you
to overhear my prayers,
let me not be afraid to dream great dreams

to pray great prayers.
With only you to hear,
I can be as bold as I need to be,
as courageous as my dreams permit,
as faithful as your love for me demands.

I want to do more than admire your saints;
I want to be one of them.

Let me not sin by hoping for too little.

If I have you, God,
my prayers will be heard,
my dreams realized.
I will want for nothing.
You alone suffice.

DAY TWENTY-ONE

....

My Day Begins

Our Lord, in order to console me,
once told me not to be distressed by the fact
that the life of the spirit
does not continue on an even path.
At one time I am fervent,
at another I am not.
At one moment I am disquieted,
a moment later I am at peace.
At still another I am tempted.
But I must, God reminded me,
hope and not fear.

We do not understand our own needs
or what we should ask for.
Let us leave all to our Lord
who knows us better than we know ourselves.
A humble heart is content with what is given it,
and does not expect special favors
as though they were a right.

But what shall I do, Lord,
if for a long time
there is no consolation at all in my prayers
and I find it almost impossible to seek you out?

I believe that the best course
is to be absolutely resigned,
confessing that we can do nothing,
and to apply ourselves to other
good and meritorious deeds.
Maybe our Lord takes away from our souls
the grace to pray easily,
so that we can learn how little it is
that we can accomplish
with only our own strength.
Rejoice and take comfort
and consider how great a privilege it is
to work in the garden of so great a Lord.

All Through the Day

It is all right to feel helpless.

My Day Is Ending

Let nothing, O Lord,
disturb the silence of this night.
Let nothing make me afraid.
However this day has gone,
let me be neither discouraged
nor presumptuous.
The life of the spirit
is not an even path.
We do not know what is good for us,
what we should ask for on any given day,
at any given moment.
Whether we are fervent or disquieted,
at peace or thrown about by temptation,
caught up in prayer or speechless,
matters not at all.
What matters is,
however my day has gone,
however I find myself as darkness comes,
that I should without ceasing
hope in you and fear not.
For if I have you, God,
I will want for nothing.
You alone suffice.

My Day Begins

Once when I was at prayer,
I saw myself on a wide plain.
I was alone in the middle of a horde
that hemmed me in on every side.
They were armed with spears and swords,
with daggers and rapiers,
prepared, it seemed to me,
and ready to hurt me.
I could not move in any direction
without exposing myself to death.
I was alone, without anyone to take my part.
In my distress, not knowing what else to do,
I lifted up my eyes to heaven
and saw Christ,
not in heaven but high above me in the air,
holding out his hand to me
and protecting me in such a way
that I was no longer afraid of those who
surrounded me.

They could not, however much they wished to do so,
cause me any harm.

At first I did not understand.
But not long afterward,
I found myself exposed to a similar assault,
and I realized that the vision
represented the world taking up arms
against my poor soul.
As in the vision,
I found myself surrounded on every side
so that I could do nothing
but lift up my eyes to heaven
and cry out to God.
I recalled the vision and I remembered
that no one can be relied upon other than God.
In all my great trials,
our Lord has always sent someone to help me,
as it was shown in the vision,
so that I might attach myself to nothing or no one,
but only try to please our Lord.

ALL THROUGH THE DAY

God alone suffices.

My Day Is Ending

Let nothing, O Lord,
disturb the silence of this night.
Let nothing make me afraid.
For in any moment of trial
you, my Lord God,
will always send someone to help me.
I can depend on you.
You are always there.
Whether surrounded on every side
or torn from within,
knowing that I can do nothing by myself,
I can still lift up my eyes to heaven
and cry out to you.
Let me come to the end of this day
welcoming the darkness in peace,
knowing that I have nothing to fear.
For if I have you, God,
I will want for nothing.
You alone suffice.

DAY TWENTY-THREE

....

MY DAY BEGINS

There is no danger, my brothers and sisters,
that when you say to God,
"thy will be done,"
you will be showered
with riches, or pleasures, or great honors,
or any earthly good.
God's love for you is not so lukewarm.
God places a higher value on your gift,
wishing to reward you generously,
since you have been given a share
in the heavenly kingdom
even in this life.

Would you like to see how God treats those
who say this prayer without reservation?
Ask Jesus,
who in the garden
uttered it truthfully and resolutely.

You will see my brothers and sisters, what God gives to
those he loves best.

See the prayer of Jesus answered
with trials, with sufferings, insults, and persecutions,
until at last
his life ended on the cross.

These are heaven's gifts in this world,
and God grants them
as a sign of affection for us—
to each of us
according to the courage and the love
we bear for God.

Fervent love can suffer much,
tepidity very little.
For my part, I believe that
our love is the measure of the cross we bear.

All Through the Day

Let me not forget
how God answered the prayers of his own son.

MY DAY IS ENDING

Let nothing, O Lord,
disturb the silence of this night.
Let nothing make me afraid.
And as this day ends,
let me not be afraid to pray
that your will be done in my life.
But let me not say this prayer too easily,
forgetting how you answered the prayers
of your own son.
I should not expect a shower
of riches, or pleasures, or great honors,
or any earthly good.
Rather you may reward me
as your rewarded your Son.
Even so, my heavenly Father,
"not my will, but yours be done."
For if I have you, God,
I can pray without fear.
You alone suffice.

DAY TWENTY-FOUR

....

My Day Begins

If you have not yet begun to meditate,
I implore you by the love of our Lord
not to deprive yourself of so great a good.
There is nothing to be afraid of;
there is everything to hope for.
You may not become perfect overnight,
or be instantly blessed
with the joys and consolations
of the great saints,
but little by little
you will grow in knowledge
of the road that leads to heaven.
Mental prayer is nothing else
but being on terms of friendship with God,
frequently conversing in secret with one
we know loves us.
Anyone who perseveres
in seeking God's friendship
is amply rewarded.

Do not make the mistake of believing
that prayer consists in much thinking,
or that we are automatically spiritual people
if we are able to think at great length about God,
or that we have failed if we cannot do so.
If you are given the grace of deep thought
and understanding, be grateful.

But if you are like me,
I have no advice to give but to be patient
until our Lord sends you both matter and light.
Place yourself in the presence of God,
and do not exhaust yourself
searching for reasons
for understanding what lies beyond your reach.
Do not lay blame on your soul,
for the good of your soul
consists not in thinking much,
but in loving much.

ALL THROUGH THE DAY

Let nothing make me afraid.

MY DAY IS ENDING

Let nothing, O Lord,
disturb the silence of this night.
And here in the gathering darkness
let me relax in your presence.
There is nothing to be afraid of.
There is everything to hope for.
I may not become perfect overnight,
or be instantly blessed
with the joys and consolations
of the great saints,
but little by little
I will grow in knowledge
of the road that leads to heaven.
Remind me that here
in the closing moments of this day,
I am in your presence.
I do not need to court you
with great thoughts or profound insights,
for the good of my soul
consists not in thinking much,
but in loving much.
If I love you, God,
I will want for nothing.
You alone suffice.

DAY TWENTY-FIVE

··

MY DAY BEGINS

If we were to live a thousand years,
we would never fully understand
how we ought to behave toward God.
In God's presence even the angels tremble—
they who can do all that God wills,
and for whom simply to wish is to accomplish.
Therefore before you pray,
stop for a moment and recall
whose presence you are approaching
and to whom you are about to speak.

If we come to prayer
ignoring whom we are addressing,
what it is that we are doing,
who it is that dares to speak with God,
then no matter what words our lips utter
we will not be praying.
It will not always be necessary
because of long practice
to consider all these things every time we pray,

but on the other hand, if we speak with God
caring not whether our words are suitable
but simply mouthing the first things
that come to mind out of rote and frequent repetition,
neither can this be called prayer.

In order to meditate you may need a book.
(For more than fourteen years
I could not meditate without reading!)
You may need to recite vocal prayers
to capture and hold your attention.
I know a sister who cannot achieve mental prayer.
She can only pause a little,
now and then,
while she says her *Paters* and *Aves*.
It is important to understand
that our father does not lead us all
by the same routes.
Those who may seem to be the least blessed of all,
may be the highest in God's eyes.

All Through the Day

Let me not forget to whom
and in whose presence
I am praying.

MY DAY IS ENDING

Let nothing, O Lord,
disturb the silence of this night
or my desire to come before you.
Let me not be overwhelmed by your presence,
silenced by my frailty,
or reduced as I so often am
to muttering familiar phrases
to overcome my speechlessness.

Accept me as I am
with what I have to give.
Heavenly Father,
you do not lead us all by the same path.
Here in your presence,
take my yearning to speak with you
and what words I have,
and make of them a prayer
worthy of your love for me.
If I have you, God,
I will want for nothing.
You alone suffice.

DAY TWENTY-SIX

My Day Begins

One day I heard these words:
"During this life, true gain consists
not in striving after greater joy in me,
but in doing my will."

My brothers and sisters, let the will of God,
to whom we belong, be achieved in our lives.
This means surrendering our life into the
hands of God,
doing what is best with our gift,
forgetting as far as possible all our self-interest,
and resigning ourselves entirely.
To truly serve God is to forget ourselves,
our advantages, our comfort,
and our apparent happiness.

The point is that we should make a gift
of our heart,
emptying it of ourselves
that it may be filled with God.

What power lies in this gift!
Our almighty father becomes one with us
and transforms us,
uniting creator and creature.

How desirable is this union!
To attain it is to live in this world and in the next
without care of any kind.
There is no secret, occult, or mysterious formula.
Our whole welfare consists solely
in doing the will of God.
But God will not force our will.
God will take only what we give.
But God will not be ours entirely
until we yield ourselves entirely to God.

ALL THROUGH THE DAY

Let the will of God be achieved in my life.

MY DAY IS ENDING

Let nothing, O Lord,
disturb the silence of this night.
Help me to take courage

from your loving presence
in the darkness gathering about me
at the end of still another day.
Let me not be afraid
to join my life with yours,
to empty my heart,
to make room for you.

You will not force your presence on me.
You go only where you are invited
and made welcome.
To make a complete gift of my heart to you,
I need more courage than I have,
strength that only you can give.

Hear my prayer.

If I have you, God,
I will want for nothing.
You alone suffice.

DAY TWENTY-SEVEN

....

MY DAY BEGINS

As for me, given a choice
I would always choose the way of suffering,
not just because it allows me to imitate the way of
Jesus,
but because it brings many other blessings with it.
We cannot understand how suffering can be a grace
and how great a blessing it is
until we have left all things for the sake of Jesus.
For if we are attached to any one thing,
it is because we set a value on it.
It may be painful to surrender what we value,
but what greater loss, what greater blindness,
what greater calamity could there be
than to make much of what is nothing,
to cling to what has no value?

One day my Lord said to me:
"Believe me, my daughter,
trials are the heaviest for those
my father loves the best.

Trials are God's measure of love.
How could I better demonstrate my love for you
than by desiring for you what I desired for myself?"

To be truly spiritual
is to make of ourselves slaves of God
branded with the cross.

God can give us no greater grace
than to give us a life
such as was led by Jesus.

All Through the Day

Trials are the measure of God's love.

My Day Is Ending

Let nothing, O Lord,
disturb the silence of this night.
In this quiet let me begin
to let go of the thousand trivial attachments
upon which I have come to depend,
out of which I have built my life,
and upon which I have rested my hopes.

Letting go of what I have come to value
will be painful.
But what greater loss could I know,
what greater blindness,
what greater calamity could there be,
than to make much of what is nothing,
to cling to what has no value?

But if I do let go,
I will have you, God,
I will want for nothing.
You alone suffice.

DAY TWENTY-EIGHT

....

My Day Begins

My love of and trust in our Lord
has never ceased to grow
from that moment when I first realized
that though he was God, he was also human.
He is not surprised
by our frailties or our continuous failures.
I can speak to him as a friend,
for though he is my Lord,
I do not consider him as one of our earthly lords,
who affect a power they do not possess,
who give audiences only at fixed times,
and to whom only certain people can speak.
If a poor person has any business with them,
it takes many approaches,
currying favor with go-betweens,
and much pain and labor before,
if ever, they gain a hearing.
But, my Lord, we do not need aides
to introduce us into your presence!
How good is our God.

How good is our Lord,
and how powerful!
You are a true friend,
and with you
I feel myself so empowered.
Knowing you will never fail me,
I feel able to withstand the whole world,
should it turn against me.
You are on our side, O Lord,
you can do all things
and subject all things to yourself.
We have nothing to fear
if we walk in the truth,
in the sight of your majesty
with a pure conscience.

ALL THROUGH THE DAY

God is a friend, my one true friend.

MY DAY IS ENDING

Let nothing, O Lord,
disturb the silence of this night.
Let me not be afraid

to linger here in your presence
with all my humanity exposed.
For you are God—
you are not surprised
by my frailties,
my continuous failures.
You are my God,
but you are also my friend.
You are on my side;
you will never fail me.
Here in the gathering darkness
I feel able to withstand the whole world,
should it turn against me.

For if I have you, God,
I want for nothing.
You alone suffice.

My Day Begins

There are moments when I wish
I had a thousand lives to spend for God,
when no penance or suffering seems too severe.
And often when the opportunity occurs
to act on these desires, they prove genuine.
But I cannot say that these desires stay with me,
for at times my soul turns coward
in the most trivial matters
and is too frightened
to undertake any work for God.

Has this not happened to you?

Sometimes I feel completely detached,
when I am in a moment of trial.
Yet the next day I discover
that I am quite attached to the very things
that I would have laughed at yesterday,
and I hardly recognize myself.

One day I am so full of courage
that I would do anything for God.
The next day I would not kill an ant
if I met the slightest opposition.
There are days when nothing anyone says disturbs me.
And yet there are also days
when a single word so devastates me
that I long to flee this world.

You, my God, know how it is.

Have pity on me.
Grant that I might accomplish
some of my dreams
for your greater honor and glory.
Spare me not completely.
For with your strength I can endure much;
without you I can do nothing.

ALL THROUGH THE DAY

God alone never changes.

MY DAY IS ENDING

Let nothing, O Lord,
disturb the silence of this night.
It is easy
here by myself,
wrapped around by your presence
to promise you the world
and my whole heart,
but by tomorrow
I may be a coward again,
clutching desperately to the things
that tonight have no importance.
Take pity on me,
even as I say my brave, generous prayers.
Grant that I might accomplish,
for your greater honor and glory,
at least some of my dreams
and overcome some of my cowardice.
For deep within my heart and soul
I desire only you, God.
You alone suffice.

DAY THIRTY

My Day Begins

My God,
you who are charity and love itself.
Help me to love myself in you,
for you and by you,
and my neighbor for your sake.
May I possess you as my sole treasure
and my one glory,
far dearer than all creatures.
Grant that I may rejoice
in your perfect love for me,
and in the eternal love borne for you
by all the angels and saints
who see you face to face.

Grant that my neighbors
may be able to bear their burdens
as I wish to bear mine.
Let them care for nothing but you,
and only for those things
that will lead them to you.

Above all else,
help me always to remember
that I have only one soul,
that I have only one short life
that must be lived
by me alone,
that I have only one death to die,
and that there is only one glory
that is eternal.

If I do this,
as you have promised,
there will be many things
I will not care about at all.

Nothing will disturb me.

ALL THROUGH THE DAY

For me to live is Christ,
to die is gain.

MY DAY IS ENDING

O Lord,
in the silence of this night,
let me hear the voice of my neighbors,
so often drowned out
by the clamor of my own needs.
Let me not fool myself into thinking
that I can hear your voice
if I do not listen to theirs.
You speak to me in the voice of my neighbors.
I cannot claim to love you
if I do not love them
even as I love myself.
Help them, I pray,
to carry their burdens,
even as I hope, with your help,
to carry mine.

You have promised,
that there will be many things
we will not care about at all,
that nothing will disturb us.
For if we have you, God,
we will want for nothing.
You alone suffice.

ONE FINAL WORD

This book was created to be nothing more than a gateway—a gateway to the spiritual wisdom of a specific teacher, and a gateway opening on your own spiritual path.

You may decide that Teresa of Avila is someone whose experience of God is one that you wish to follow more closely and deeply. In that case, you should read more. There is no shortage of material by and about this extraordinary mystic and practitioner of the spiritual life. Her own works, including her autobiography, fill several volumes. And for centuries, scholars and mystics have written about her teachings and edited her works for easier access.

You may decide that her experience has not helped you. There are many other teachers. Somewhere there is the right teacher for your own, very special, absolutely unique journey of the spirit. You *will* find your teacher; you *will* discover your path.

We would not be searching, as St. Augustine reminds us, if we had not already been found.

One more thing should be said.

Spirituality is not meant to be self-absorption, a cocoon-like relationship of "God and me." In the long run, if it is to have meaning, if it is to grow and not wither, it must be a wellspring of compassionate living. It must reach out to others as God has reached out to us. True spirituality breaks down the walls of our souls and lets in not just heaven, but the whole world.

30 Days with a
GREAT SPIRITUAL TEACHER
Series

Each book in the 30 Days with a Great Spiritual Teacher series provides a month of daily readings from one of Christianity's most beloved spiritual guides.

Simply Surrender
Thérèse of Lisieux
ISBN: 9781594711541
128 pages / $9.95

Set Your Heart Free
Francis de Sales
ISBN: 9781594711534
120 pages / $9.95

Let Nothing Disturb You
Teresa of Avila
ISBN: 9781594711527
120 pages / $9.95

All Will Be Well
Julian of Norwich
ISBN: 9781594711510
128 pages / $9.95

You Shall Not Want
The Psalms
ISBN: 9781594711565
120 pages / $9.95

Peace of Heart
Francis of Assisi
ISBN: 9781594711558
128 pages / $9.95

AVE

Available from your local bookstore or from
ave maria press / Notre Dame, IN 46556
www.avemariapress.com / Ph: 800-282-1865
A Ministry of the United States Province of Holy Cross

Keycode: FD912Ø7ØØØØ